NOW I KNOW™
Baby Anima

by MELVIN AND GILDA BERGER

SCHOLASTIC INC.

New York   Toronto   London   Auckland   Sydney
Mexico City   New Delhi   Hong Kong   Buenos Aires

ISBN-13: 978-0-439-92387-3
ISBN-10: 0-439-92387-5

12 11 10 9 8 7 6 5 4 3   10 11 12/0

Printed in the U.S.A.
First Printing, March 2007

Can you find the baby animals?

A baby cat is called a kitten.

A baby deer is called a fawn.

A puppy is a baby dog.

A lamb is a baby sheep.

ZOOM!

What do baby animals eat?
Some drink their mother's milk.

Some eat other foods.

Newborn rabbits are very little.

Elephant babies are very big.

A baby gorilla rides on
its mother's back.

DID YOU KNOW?
Baby swans are called cygnets (SIG-nits).

So does a baby swan.

Who keeps baby elephants safe?

DID YOU KNOW?

A grown giraffe is almost as tall as a two-story building!

Who watches over baby giraffes?
Their parents do!

15

Animal babies get lots of love.

A seal mother and baby rub noses.

Chimpanzees hug
and kiss.

Chimpanzees clean each
other — and their babies.

DID YOU KNOW?
Cats and tigers
are in the same
family.

A mother tiger licks her baby.

20

A mother pig and her piglet
take a cool mud bath.

A colt learns to run.

A baby bird learns to fly.

A baby dolphin learns to jump.

What does a baby bear learn to do?

Many baby animals like to play.

Puppies have fun with a bone.

DID YOU KNOW?
A baby
kangaroo
is called a joey.

Some babies stay with their
mothers for many months.

Others stay for years.

Baby animals grow up—and leave.

One day they have babies
of their own.

GLOSSARY

Animal: A living creature that can breathe and move about.

Baby: A very young animal or child.

Colt: A baby male horse. A baby female horse is called a filly.

Cygnet: A baby swan.

Fawn: A baby deer.

Joey: A baby kangaroo.

Kit: A baby rabbit.

Kitten: A baby cat.

Lamb: A baby sheep.

Piglet: A baby pig or hog.

Puppy: A baby dog.